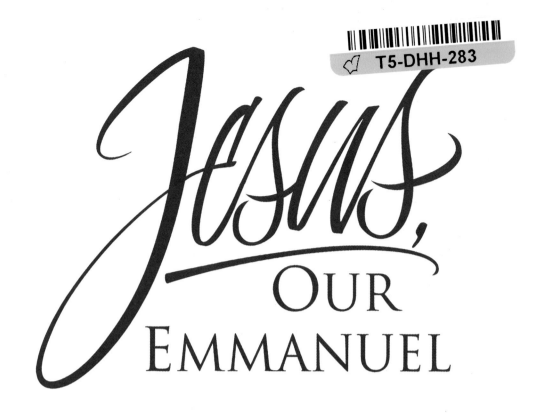

Jesus, OUR EMMANUEL

THE PRESENCE OF GOD... WITH US

A Christmas Musical

WRITTEN AND ARRANGED BY MARTY PARKS

Lillenas PUBLISHING COMPANY

KANSAS CITY, MO 64141

www.lillenas.com

8. 3

CONTENTS

Hark! the Herald Angels Sing

CHARLES WESLEY

FELIX MENDELSSOHN
Arranged by Marty Parks

heav'n a - dored!_____ Christ, the ev - er - last - ing

F2   Dm   Gm   F/C   C7

Lord!   Late in time be - hold Him come-_____

Unison

F2

CD: 5

Off - spring of the Vir - gin's womb.

Divisi

Am7   G/B   C   C/G   G7   C2   C/E

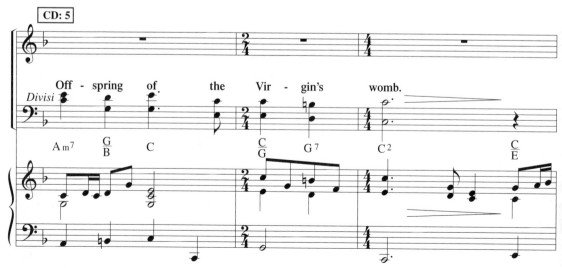

12

NARRATOR I: Christmas is a message from the heart of God to the heart of mankind. The message of Christmas is one so personal it could never be entrusted to another messenger. No, God Himself must deliver the astounding news that He, majestic and holy, desires fellowship...with us.

NARRATOR II: The message began centuries ago when the Creator spoke to Moses in the wilderness, instructing him to build a tabernacle. "That is where I will meet you," God said. And down through the ages He chose to make His presence known among His people; sometimes quietly, sometimes in great power. And where His presence was known, lives were changed.

(music begins)

NARRATOR I: Finally, in one dramatic, unthinkable gesture, the God of eternity chose to be among us, as one of us. He was exactly what we needed then; He is precisely what we're needing now.

NARRATOR II: We dare not speak thoughtless words in His presence. Even heaven's armies stand in hushed amazement at the grand mystery of the incarnation. We can only respond softly from our hearts: "Alleluia, alleluia."

Jesus, Our Emmanuel

with
Let All Mortal Flesh Keep Silence

Words and Music by
MARTY PARKS
Arranged by Marty Parks

Choir unison

23 *mp*

hand. Christ, Our God to earth de-

scend - eth, Our full hom - age to de-

CD: 10

mand.

28 *Men unison*
mp

At His feet the six - winged_____ ser - aph,

CD: 12

Je - sus, our Em-man - u - el.

Em   G/A   A   G/A   D   G/A

50 *Choir unison (soloist continues)*
mf

Je - sus, our Em-man - u - el.

D   D/F♯   G2   G

Je - sus, our Em-man - u - el.

Em   Em/G   A2   A   A/G

54

We need Your pres - ence more than we could ev - er tell,

F♯m   Bm7   Em   D/F♯   G2   G

CD: 14

(music begins)

NARRATOR I: The wonderful reality of the Christmas message is this: The God who desires to be with us, knows us. Each of us! By name and individually.

NARRATOR II: So it was with a young virgin named Mary. God's angel greeted her with honor: "Hail, favored one! The Lord is with you!" From among all people, the Almighty had chosen her. She would become the mother of God's own Son.

NARRATOR I: Impossible? Not with God. Nothing is impossible with Him. Mary's soul burst out in a song of praise to her God. And Mary's song has become our song: "Proclaim His greatness! He has done wonderful things!"

My Soul Proclaims the Greatness of the Lord

includes
Holy, Holy, Holy! Lord God Almighty

Words and Music by
MARTY PARKS
Arranged by Marty Parks

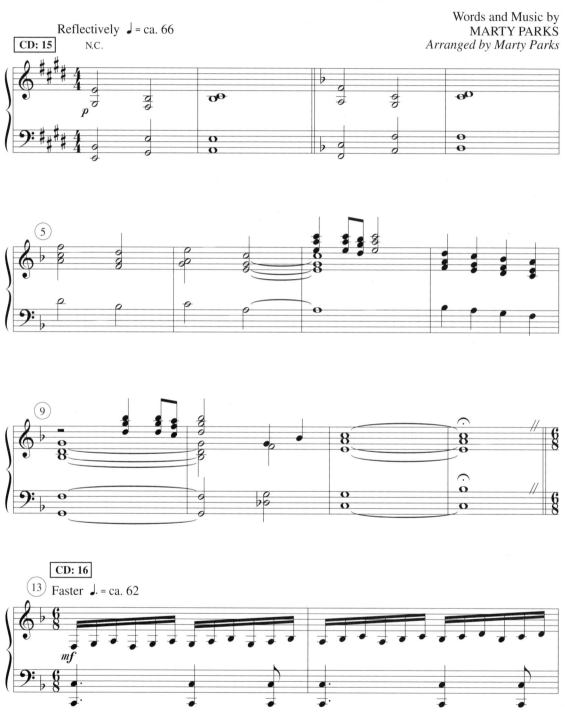

My soul pro-claims the great-ness of the

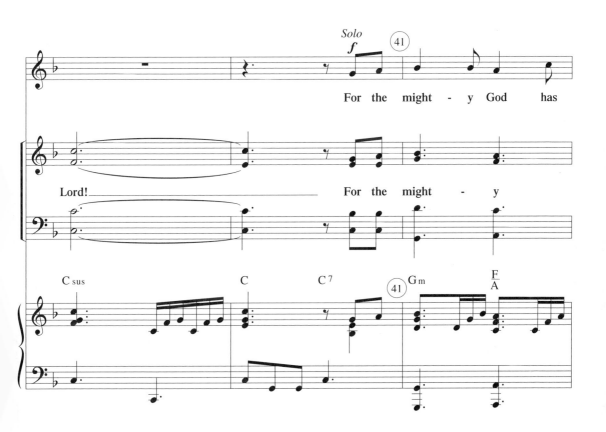

For the might - y God has

Lord! For the might - y

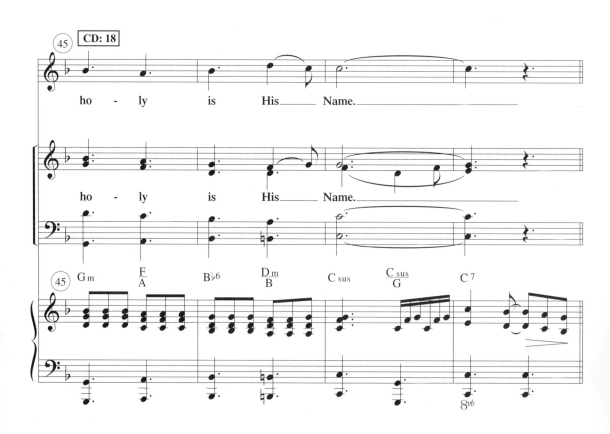

34

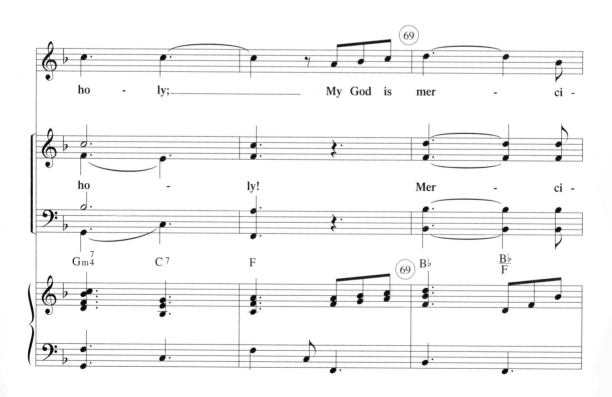

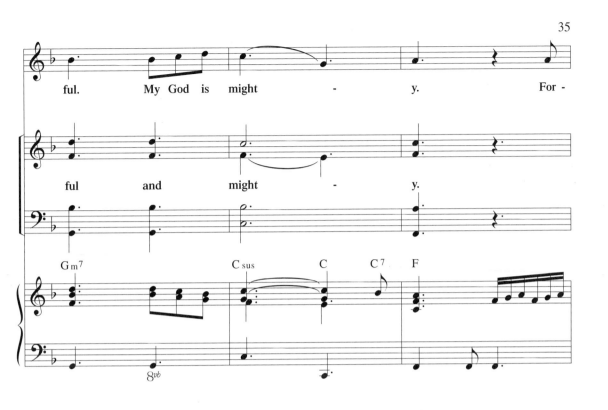

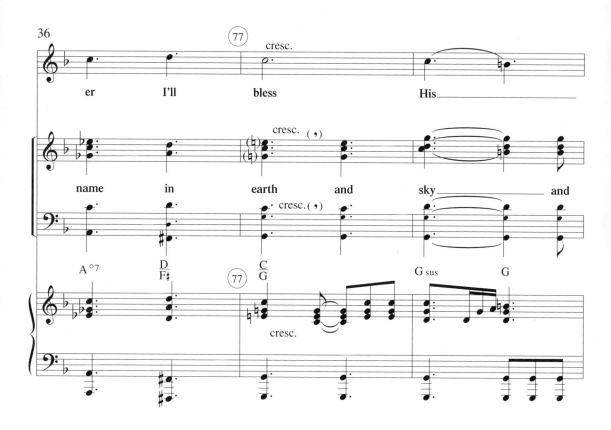

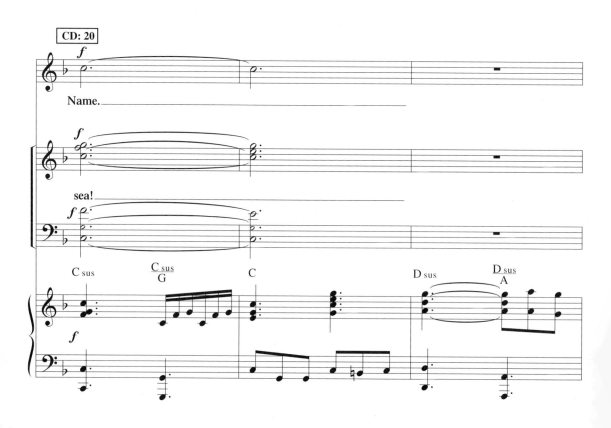

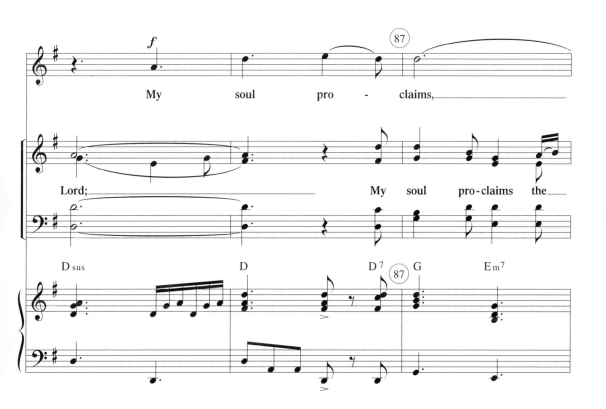

38

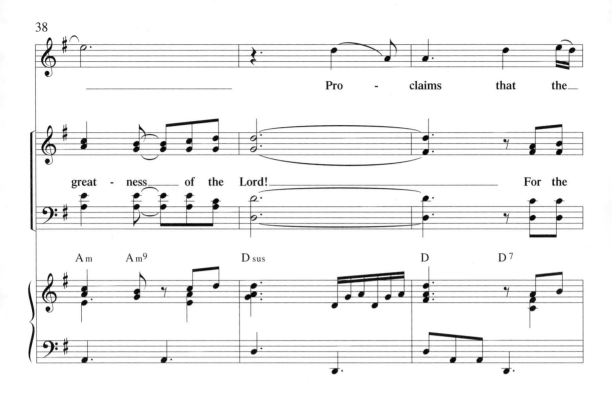

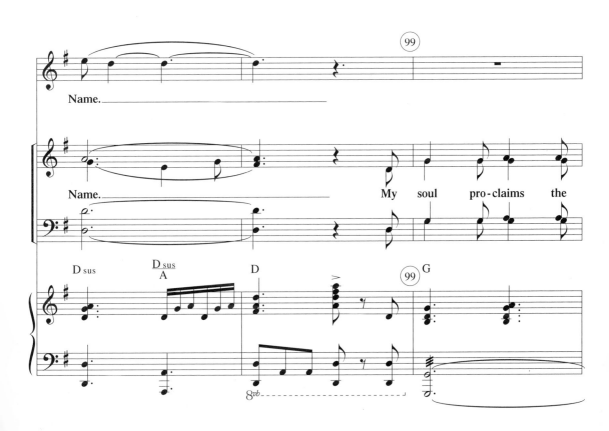

40

NARRATOR II: The mystery of the incarnation is beyond our understanding. It is broader than our imagination and it is outside the scope of our experience. The presence of God has always evoked wonder and delight; reverence and fear.

NARRATOR I: He appeared in the temple worship of Solomon and in the transcendent vision of Isaiah. Then after decades of silence, He made Himself known on a quiet hillside outside Bethlehem. A dazzling array of angels lit up the countryside. A startled band of shepherds was engulfed in the glory of Almighty God and their lives would be changed forever.

NARRATOR II: A new day was dawning. *(music begins)* A new age was being ushered in, the likes of which we'd never seen before. Suddenly, the whole earth was an unwitting host to the presence of God Himself...God with us!

Christ Is Born! Sing Alleluia!

includes
How Great Our Joy

Words and Music by
MARTY PARKS
Arranged by Marty Parks

44

46

49

50

He's born! Christ is born!

Prince of Peace. Christ is born! Sing

Unison *Divisi*

CD: 28

Al - le - lu - ia!

(ah) Al - le - lu - ia!

Christ is___ born!___

Al - le - lu - ia!___

D   Bm7 F#m   E   A

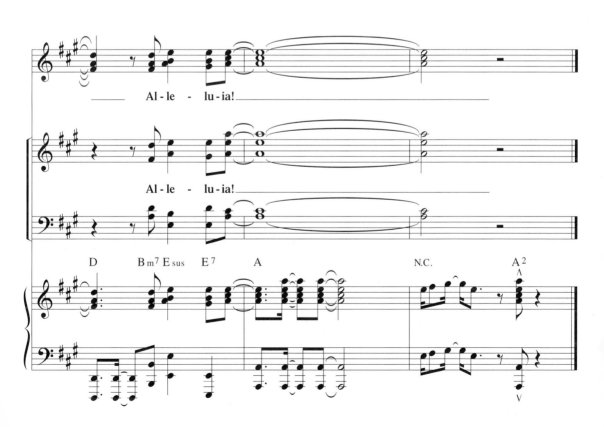

___ Al - le - lu - ia!___

Al - le - lu - ia!___

D   Bm7 Esus E7   A   N.C.   A2

Gloria in Excelsis Deo

Words and Music by
MARTY PARKS
Arranged by Marty Parks

56

CD: 34

NARRATOR I: Though unrestricted by time itself, God selected just the right moment for the birth of His Son. His timing, as always, was perfect.

NARRATOR II: The Roman empire held undisputed world dominance, establishing a network of civilization that would provide for the spreading of the gospel of Christ. The Greek language was nearly universal, understood by commoner and philosopher alike, and was beautifully suited to an accurate presentation of the Christian message.

NARRATOR I: According to both pagan and Jewish writings of the day, most of the world's inhabitants were longing for something to lift them from the moral and spiritual decay around them. *(music begins)* Most importantly, God's prophetic timetable was pointing to the most significant event history had ever known.

NARRATOR II: The One who transcends time and space became bound by both. The Creator became the created. In the fulness of time, the Sovereign Lord who reigns in heaven's splendor, elected to dwell...with us.

NARRATOR I: The Word became flesh.

And the Word Became Flesh

Based on John 1

MARTY PARKS
Arranged by Marty Parks

62

Word was with God, And the Word was God.

Word, And the Word was with God, And the

Word was God.

Ladies unison
mp

In Him was life, and that

63

64

65

66

seen the glo-ry of the Fath - er, Re -
vealed in Christ, the Son: The One and on - ly.
Je - sus!

70

NARRATOR I: To the ancient people of faith, names were often a
reflecton of some future purpose or some significant event in the
past. And when God revealed His names, all who listened could
hear of the incredible aspects of His character.

NARRATOR II: He is El Shaddai - God Almighty; Jehovah Rapha - the
God who heals; Elohim - the Creator; Jehovah Jireh - the God
who provides; He is El Elyon - God Most High.

(music begins)

NARRATOR I: Mary and Joseph did not have the privilege of naming their
infant Son. The angel had clearly told them, "You are to give
Him the name Jesus."

NARRATOR II: Long before this, however, the Father had spoken through
His prophets that a virgin would be with child and give birth to a
son...she would name Him Emmanuel. It's a name that speaks
directly to our deepest need; a name that brings hope to a
desperate world; a name that forever defines God's relentless
quest to bring us to Him. Emmanuel, God with us.

One Name Says It All

Words and Music by
MARTY PARKS
Arranged by Marty Parks

15 *Ladies unison*
mp

What would it take_____ when you think where we've been,_____

D sus   D m   G m2   G m

What would it take_____ to bring us back home a - gain?_____

A7sus   A7   G m   D m   C2   F

19

In all our dark - ness, in all our night,_____ How

D m   D sus / C   D m / C   G 4/2   G 9

CD: 45

can we re-turn_____ to the light?_____

B♭m(M7)/G   B♭m6/D♭   B♭m6/C   N.C.   G m7/C   C 7

CD: 46

78

82

NARRATOR II: How totally like God to surprise us with His coming. He filled the earth with the glory of His presence, but announced His arrival in unexpected ways. Oh, there had been signs and prophecies all along. But when He finally appeared, only a handful even noticed. A group of shepherds, outcasts really, were assured that to them a Savior had been born. And a very knowledgeable group of seekers were led on an amazing journey by a single mysterious star.

NARRATOR I: We don't know much about these Wise Men except what's most important. Their longing for truth compelled them to leave their own country in search of the Source of truth. And when they found Him, they fell down in adoration. One thing is certain: this was no timid, reserved spiritual observance. This was exuberant worship from the depths of their souls! A star had led them to the Sovereign of the universe, and they were overjoyed.

(music begins)

NARRATOR II: "Let the hearts of those who seek the Lord rejoice." That's what the Psalmist said and that's what the Wise Men experienced. But beyond their experience, they've shown us how to discover for ourselves a Savior.

Come to the Light

Words and Music by
MARTY PARKS
Arranged by Marty Parks

86

88

90

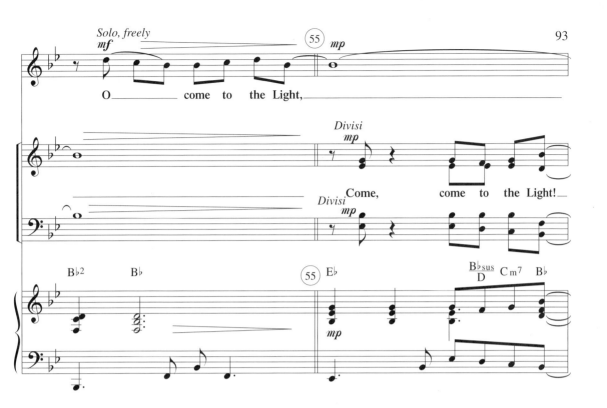

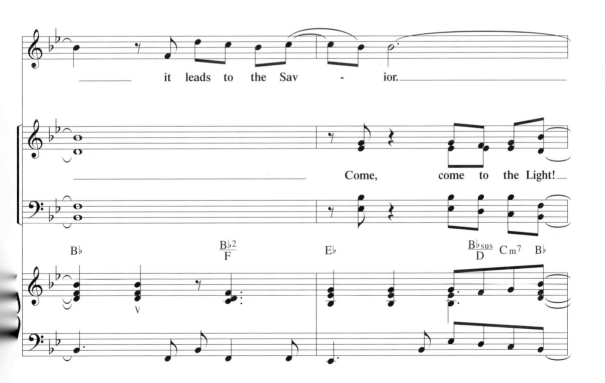

94

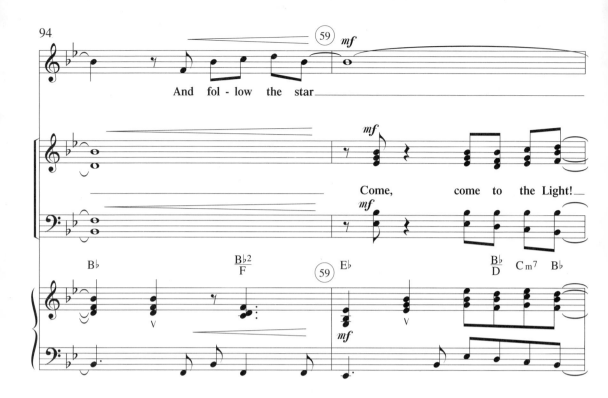

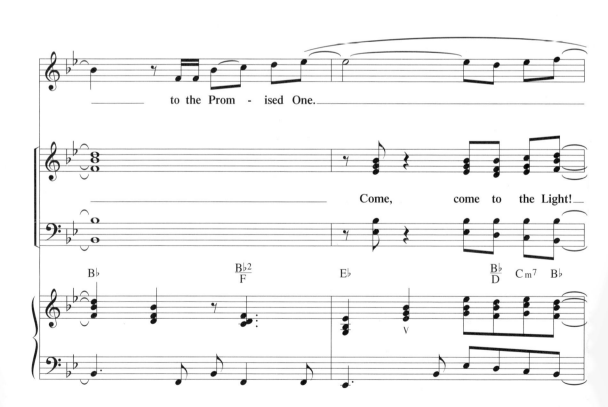

CD: 56

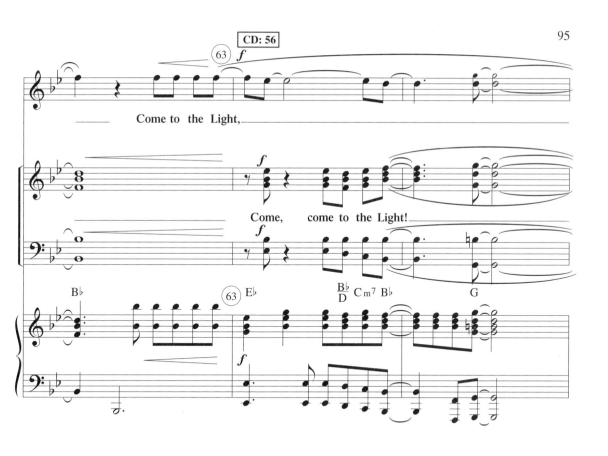

Come to the Light,

Come, come to the Light!

B♭   E♭   B♭/D C m7 B♭   G

Be-hold the glo - ry,

Be-hold the glo - ry, the won-drous sto - ry,

G   G sus/A G/B   Cm   B♭/D   Cm   B♭/D

96

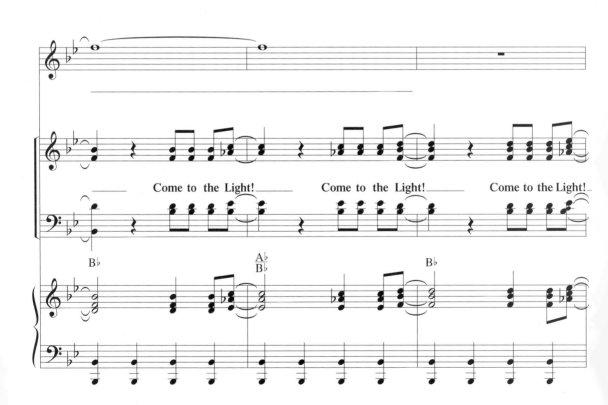

Come to the Light!_____ Come to the Light!_

_____ Come to the Light!

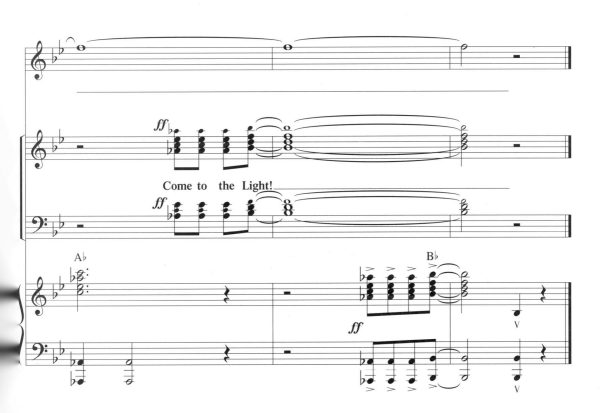

Come to the Light!_

O the Glory of Your Presence

with

O Little Town of Bethlehem

Words and Music by
STEVE FRY
Arranged by Marty Parks

Gently ♩= ca. 72

CD: 57

*NARRATOR I : Let's pray. Lord Jesus, we stand in utter amazement that You
would honor us by coming to be among us and be one of us. More than anything
we want to know once again the glory of Your presence. We want the story of Your
birth to be the story of our rebirth. We want the adoration of the Wise Men to be our
life-song of devotion. We want the undeniable truth of Your presence to be a living
reality for us today and every day. Fill us, Lord, with Your presence.

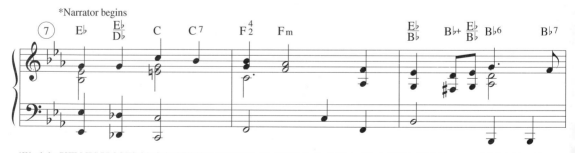

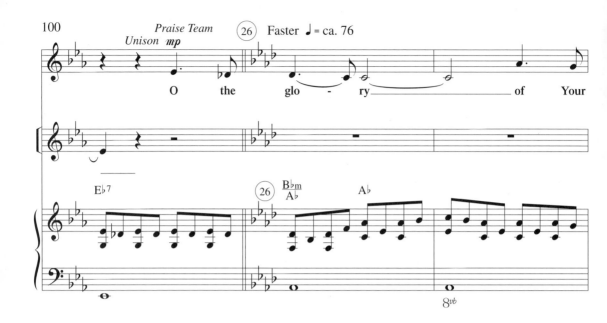

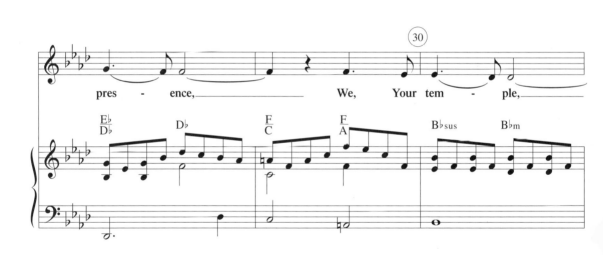

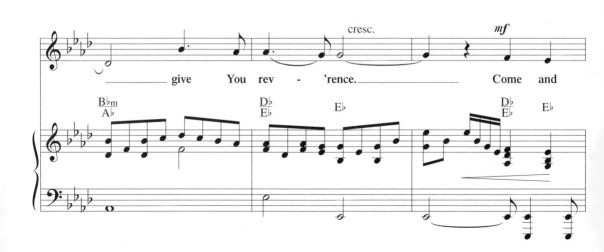

102

104

Finale

Christ Is Born! Sing Alleluia!
Come to the Light
Jesus, Our Emmanuel
Hark! the Herald Angels Sing

Arranged by Marty Parks

106

Christ is____ born!_____ The Prince of____ Peace.____

Christ is____ born!_____ Sing (ah) Al - le - lu - ia!

CD: 63

Christ is___ born!___ Al - le - lu - ia!___

Unison
Christ is___ born!___ Sing (ah) Al - le - lu - ia!

Divisi

A   A/C#   Bm7   F#m   E

CD: 64

slight rit.

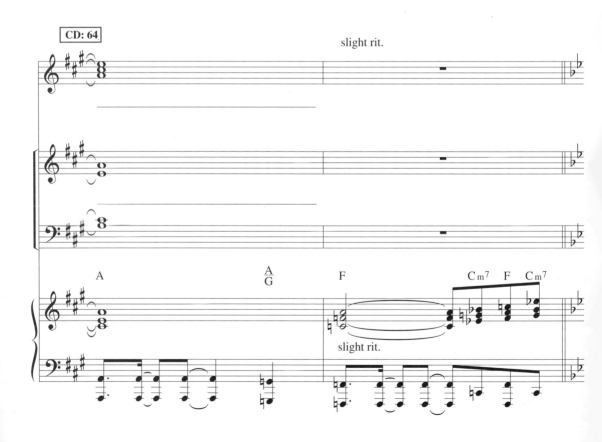

A   A/G   F   Cm7   F   Cm7

slight rit.

*"Come to the Light"

A little slower ♩ = ca. 96

Come to the Light,_____ it leads to the Sav-

-ior, Fol - low the star_____ to the Prom - ised One.___

Come to the Light_____ and wor - ship Him on -

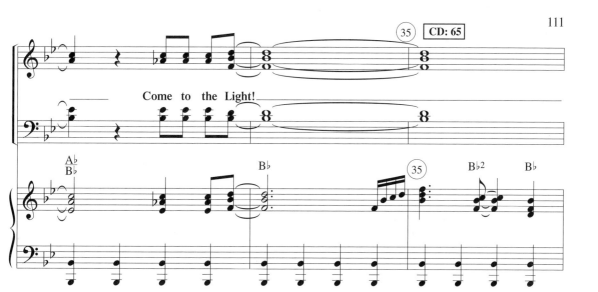

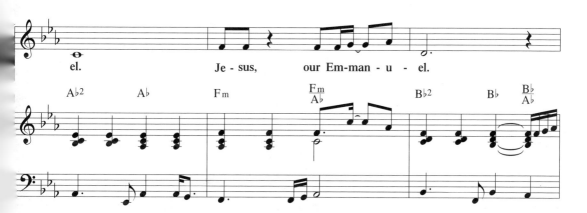

112

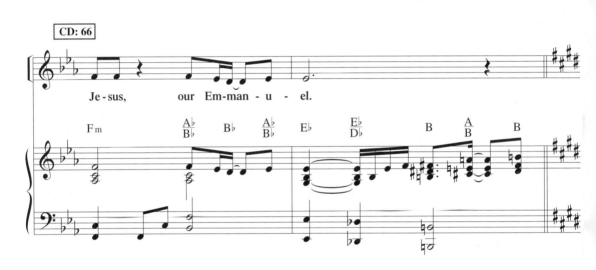

114

*"Hark! the Herald Angels Sing"

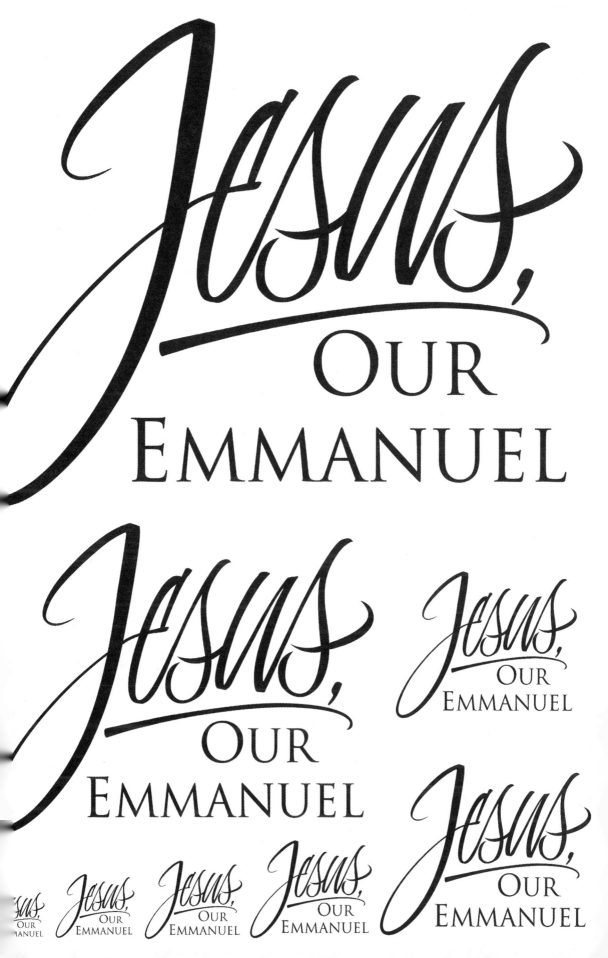